Coral Reefs
Life Below the Sea

Coral Reefs
Life Below the Sea

Salvatore Tocci

Franklin Watts
A Division of Scholastic Inc.
New York • Toronto • London • Auckland • Sydney
Mexico City • New Delhi • Hong Kong
Danbury, Connecticut

For Pete, a gentle man with whom
I wish I could have spent more time.

Note to readers: Definitions for words in **bold** can be found in the Glossary at the back of this book.

Photographs © 2004: Corbis Images: 45 bottom (Hal Beral), 6 (Bettmann), 50 (Bojan Brecelj), 28 (Amos Nachoum), 16 (Jeffrey L Rotman), 10 (Paul A. Souders), 36 fan worm (Lawson Wood); Dembinsky Photo Assoc./Patti McConville: 52; Mandy Richman: 8, 9; Minden Pictures: 20, 22, 26 (Fred Bavendam), 5 right (Chris Newbert), cover (Birgitte Wilms), 14, 23, 41 (Norbert Wu); Photo Researchers, NY: 36 angelfish (Charles Angelo), 30 (Dr. Jeremy Burgess), 45 top (B. Jones/M. Shimlock), 36 butterfly fish, 43 (Frederick R. McConnaughey), 32 top (Trevor McDonald), 36 sea slug (Newman & Flowers), 27 top (Matthew Oldfield), 15, 42 left (Peter Scoones), 13, 36 blue devil damsel (Mark Smith), 36 zooplankton (Andrew Syred); Seapics.com: 33 (Franco Banfi), 40 (Marc Bernardi) , 27 bottom, 48 (Marc Chamberlain), 2, 12, 36 coral polyps (Mark Conlin), 44 (Reinhard Dirscherl), 18, 19, 36 reef shark (David B. Fleetham), 32 bottom (Richard Herrmann), 5 left, 24, 36 tube sponge, 38 (Doug Perrine), 21 (D.R. & T.L. Schrichte), 25, 34, 36 puffer fish (Masa Ushioda); Visuals Unlimited: 42 right (Brandon Cole), 46 (David Wrobel).

The photograph on the cover shows a section of a coral reef. The photograph opposite the title page shows an aerial view of a coral reef.

Library of Congress Cataloging-in-Publication Data

Tocci, Salvatore.
    Coral reefs : life below the sea / Salvatore Tocci.
        v. cm. — (Watts library)
    Includes bibliographical references (p.   ).
    Contents: An impressive structure — Living relationships — Feeding relationships — Survival tactics — A fragile structure.
    ISBN 0-531-12304-9 (lib. bdg.)   0-531-16669-4 (pbk.)
    1. Coral reef ecology—Juvenile literature. 2. Coral reefs and islands—Juvenile literature. [1. Coral reef ecology. 2. Coral reefs and islands. 3. Ecology.] I. Title. II. Series.
QH541.5.C7T63 2003
577.7'89—dc22

2003016566

Contents

An illustration of a Spanish galleon sailing in a storm.

Lost at Sea

Throughout the long night, five men clung to the ship's mast, which was floating in the water. Their ship, the *Atocha*, had sunk the day before north of Cuba in the Atlantic Ocean. The ship went down quickly, bringing 260 people to the sea bottom with it. Only the five men floating in the water were lucky enough to escape with their lives.

The *Atocha* had set sail from Cuba on September 4, 1622. The ship was part of the Spanish navy and was heading home. The *Atocha* was carrying a fortune. Its cargo consisted of tons of silver and gold.

The Atocha struck rocks like these, which are found only in warm, tropical seas.

It also carried chests filled with precious gems, such as rubies and emeralds.

The morning the *Atocha* sailed from Cuba was beautiful. That night, however, strong winds churned up the seas and

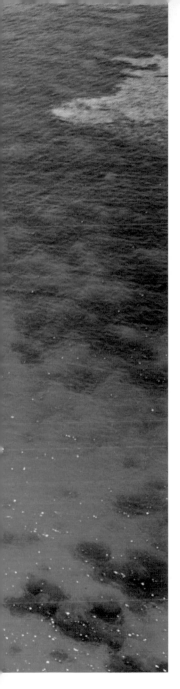

tore apart the ship's sails. Without its sails, the *Atocha* drifted helplessly. It moved more like a roller coaster than a ship, rising high on each wave and then quickly falling back down into the sea. Suddenly, its ride on the waves came to an end.

Plunging from the top of a huge wave, the *Atocha* smashed violently into a group of rocks lying just beneath the surface of the ocean. The rocks ripped open its hull, and water began to pour into the ship. There was no time for the people onboard, except for five men, to save themselves.

The *Atocha* lay at the bottom of the sea until 1985, when divers discovered the ship and recovered its treasures. For 363 years, the *Atocha* lay on the sea bottom, only 55 feet (17 meters) beneath the surface. The rocks the ship had struck are found only in warm, shallow seas.

A Valuable Jewel

One single jewel alone recovered from the *Atocha* was valued at more than $2 million.

9

The Great Barrier Reef, the world's largest coral reef, is actually made of more than three thousand smaller reefs that lie very close to one another.

Chapter One

An Impressive Structure

The rocks the *Atocha* struck are part of a **coral reef**. A coral reef is a ridge of rocky material just beneath the surface of a tropical sea that has been made by living things. This definition, however, does not convey how impressive a coral reef really is.

Part of what makes coral reefs so impressive is that they are the largest structures on Earth made by living things. One example is the Great Barrier Reef, which extends along the eastern coast of Australia for more than 1,250 miles (2,010 kilometers). This coral reef would span the entire eastern coast of the United States, stretching from Maine to Florida.

Besides being the largest structures, coral reefs are also the most spectacular structures made by living things. A coral reef is a place brimming with **organisms**, or living things, that have striking colors, strange shapes, and fascinating habits. Nowhere else in the seas do so many different organisms live so closely together.

Coral reefs are home to many kinds of colorful fish.

Coral reefs are also among the oldest structures on Earth. Some, like the Great Barrier Reef, started forming about 25 million years ago. Coral reefs first existed on Earth nearly 400 million years ago, a time when no living thing could be found on land. Exploring a coral reef today is like taking a trip back in time. Some organisms look very much like their ancestors, which lived almost 100 million years ago, during the age of dinosaurs.

This organism, which lives in coral reefs in the Pacific Ocean, looks much like its ancestors, which lived more than forty million years ago.

Value of Reefs

Coral reefs are admired for their beauty. These beautiful **habitats**, or places where organisms live, are home to an extraordinary variety of plants and animals. More than 100,000 kinds of plants and animals have been identified and described. Scientists estimate that between 500,000 and 2,000,000 types of organisms may actually inhabit coral reefs. No other habitat in the seas has the diversity of life, or **biodiversity**, that is found in a coral reef.

The biodiversity found on a coral reef has proven to be of great value to humans in several ways. For example, reefs are an important source of food for millions of people, especially those living on islands in the Pacific Ocean. More than 2.5 million people live on these islands, which are built from coral reefs or are surrounded by them. These people get much of

Many tourists snorkel or scuba dive to get a close look at a coral reef.

their food, such as fish, clams, eels, mussels, shrimps, and lobsters, from the waters surrounding these reefs.

For tens of thousands of people, coral reefs provide the only way of earning a living. Tourists spend billions of dollars each year to get a close look at the biodiversity found in a coral reef. In many reef areas, tourists outnumber residents. About one hundred countries with coral reefs get more than half their annual income from tourists. However, the value of coral reefs to humans goes far beyond the money generated through tourism.

Coral reefs are also an important source of such medicines as AZT (zidovudine), which is used to treat people who are HIV-positive. Reef organisms have also been used to develop medicines to treat infections, heart disease, and some forms of cancer. With so many reef organisms yet to be identified and studied, scientists are not sure how many more medicines might be developed from reef organisms.

Reef Builders

A coral reef is built by millions of very tiny animals known as **polyps**. Polyps belong to a group of animals that includes jellyfish. A coral polyp has a soft, round body that is about the size of a pencil eraser. A polyp feeds by using its tentacles to catch tiny organisms that swim by. The food is then moved into the polyp's hollow body, where it is digested.

Polyps usually live in large groups called colonies. A coral polyp is a **sessile** animal, which means it does not move from place to place. In fact, a polyp often remains in the same place for its entire life.

There are two types of coral polyps, hard and soft. Both types have soft bodies. However, hard coral polyps secrete a substance called calcium carbonate that collects around their bottoms. The calcium carbonate slowly hardens to form a shell into which the polyp can withdraw to seek protection. Unlike hard coral polyps, soft coral polyps do not secrete calcium carbonate.

Each coral polyp has at least six tentacles that are used to capture food.

When a hard coral polyp dies, its calcium carbonate shell remains. Another hard coral polyp may attach itself to this shell. The calcium carbonate it secretes will build up and harden on the preexisting shell. This process continues as old polyps die and new ones continue to build on the shells that are left behind. These shells gradually form the coral rocks that make up a reef.

A Slow Process

Reef building is a very slow process. The average rate of growth of a reef is only about 0.5 inches (1.25 centimeters) a

Coral polyps get their green and yellow colors from the algae that live inside them.

year. To build up a coral reef even this small amount each year, polyps need just the right conditions.

First, the water temperature must stay between 64° and 88° Fahrenheit (17° and 31° Celsius) throughout the year. For this reason, coral reefs form only in seas near the equator where the temperature does not change much throughout the year. Second, the water must contain just the right concentrations of various substances. For example, if there is not enough calcium present in the water, the polyps cannot make their hard shells. Finally, coral growth depends on sunlight. Polyps do not live below 82 feet (25 m) because not enough sunlight reaches this depth.

The sunlight is not needed by the coral polyps themselves, but rather by tiny, plantlike organisms called **algae** that live inside them. The algae are mostly green and yellow and give the polyps their bright colors. The algae need sunlight to perform **photosynthesis**. Photosynthesis is the process by which such organisms as green plants and algae make food.

Other types of algae that live outside polyps also help in the building of a coral reef. Like the polyps, these algae secrete calcium carbonate. These algae are red, pink, and white and

Worms

Most coral reefs are built by polyps. Some reefs, however, are built by other small animals, such as worms.

add to the beautiful colors seen on the three major types of reefs.

The simplest and most common type of reef is a **fringing reef**. This type of reef is fairly narrow and develops near the shore. A narrow channel of water separates a fringing reef from land.

A second type of reef is a **barrier reef**, which is found farther offshore than a fringing reef. A barrier reef forms when the landmass beneath a fringing reef sinks. As the landmass sinks, the fringing reef slowly becomes separated from the shore by a wide channel of water. The reef continues to grow farther and farther offshore, eventually becoming a barrier reef.

A third type of reef is called an **atoll**. An atoll develops from fringing reefs that form around a small island. If the island slowly sinks below the ocean surface, all that remains above the water is a ring of coral surrounding a lagoon. This ring of coral is an atoll.

Rising Offshore

A barrier reef can also rise from offshore if the seabed is shallow enough to allow coral polyps to survive.

The red dots on this map show the locations of coral reefs around the world.

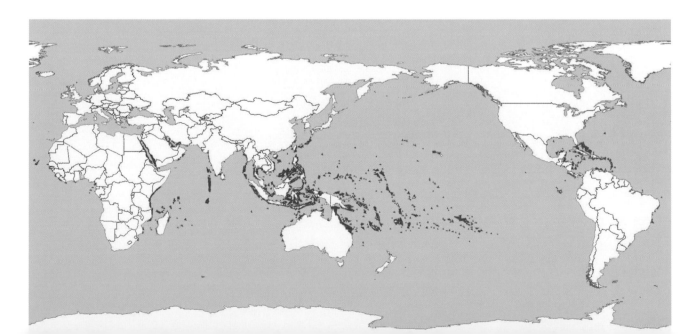

A giant clam may live for two hundred years.

Chapter Two

Living Relationships

No matter what type of coral reef they live on, many of the organisms living on reefs have developed very close relationships. For example, coral polyps depend on the algae that live inside them for food. In turn, the algae depend on the polyps for protection. In other words, both organisms benefit from one another. This type of relationship is called **mutualism**. A coral reef is a place where mutualism is a way of life.

The algae that benefit coral polyps also help other reef organisms, such as the giant clam. This animal has truly earned its name. Some giant clams grow more than 4 inches (10 cm) a year and reach a length of 2 feet (60 cm) within ten years. When fully grown, a giant clam can reach a length of 4 feet (1.2 m) and weigh more than 500 pounds (225 kilograms).

Most clams feed by filtering seawater to remove the tiny organisms in it. However, giant clams have another way of getting food. Like coral polyps, giant clams have algae living inside their bodies. These algae carry out photosynthesis to supply both themselves and the clams with food. The algae benefit by being protected from harm inside the giant clam's shell.

Another example of mutualism on a reef is displayed by the relationship between pistol shrimp and gobies, which are tiny fish that have a long, slender shape. Pistol shrimp and gobies

Algae living inside the giant clam are the source of its bright colors.

Although a moray eel may attack a diver exploring a reef, it will not harm the shrimp that clean its body.

share burrows in the reef. The gobies benefit by gobbling up some of the tiny organisms that are stunned by the shrimp. In turn, the gobies warn the shrimp of approaching danger when they retreat into their burrows and bump into the shrimp. The shrimp, which are almost blind, would be easy targets if it were not for the warning provided by the gobies.

Another shrimp with an interesting name also exhibits mutualism. This is the cleaner shrimp, whose name comes from the job it performs in a coral reef. These tiny shrimp remove and eat harmful organisms from fish and other reef organisms, such as the moray eel. Surprisingly, a moray eel,

Cleaning Stations

Groups of cleaner shrimp are often found in various spots on a coral reef. Other reef dwellers go to these places to seek the services of the cleaner shrimp. These places are known as "cleaning stations" because of the type of work done by the cleaner shrimp. Cleaning stations are scattered throughout a coral reef.

The pistol shrimp is also known as the snapping shrimp because of the sound it makes when it snaps part of its body to shoot out water.

with its huge jaws and big appetite, allows the shrimp to crawl all over its body. While the shrimp get a free meal, the eel benefits by having harmful organisms removed from its body.

Sounds and Lights

The world beneath the surface of the ocean is far from quiet. The strangest sound heard in a reef might be the crackling noise made by the pistol shrimp. This sound is made when the shrimp quickly snaps a part of its body to help spurt water from its mouth. The spurt of water is intended to stun a tiny organism that can then be captured and eaten by the shrimp.

Besides hearing strange sounds, a visitor to a coral reef may also see bright lights. This light may be coming from an animal appropriately called a flashlight fish. Inside a special structure in its body are billions of tiny organisms called bacteria. Together, these bacteria produce a powerful light. When the fish opens a pouch on the side of its body, the light can be seen

The light from a flashlight fish is the brightest light produced by any organism.

more than 100 feet (30 m) away. The light produced by the bacteria helps the fish attract food. The bacteria benefit by getting food supplied by the fish.

One-Sided Relationships

Relationships between two different reef organisms do not always involve benefits to both parties. In some cases, only one organism benefits, while the other organism is not affected in any way. Such a relationship is known as **commensalism**.

An example of commensalism can be seen in the manta ray's relationship with the suckerfish. Manta rays spend most of their time in the open seas, but they occasionally venture into coral reefs. Spotting a manta ray is easy because of its large size and the unusual way in which it moves through the water. These animals can weigh more than 3,000 pounds (1360 kg). Known as the "birds" of the sea, manta rays swim by moving their huge, winglike fins up and down. Despite

Notice the suckerfish attached to the manta ray's body. A manta ray can reach 20 feet (6 m) in width.

their fearsome look, manta rays are among the gentlest creatures of the sea. They feed on tiny organisms that they trap by filtering seawater through their mouths and gills.

A manta ray often has another animal attached to the bottom of its body that is getting a free ride. This animal is commonly known as a suckerfish because of the sucker it uses to attach itself to the manta ray. As the manta ray swims through the water and captures its food, the suckerfish picks up any scraps it can. The manta ray is not affected in any way by having the suckerfish attached to its body.

Protected by Law

The shells of giant tritons are prized by many visitors to a coral reef because of their size and beauty. Even those who live near a coral reef seek out these shells. On islands throughout the Pacific Ocean, including Hawaii, people have traditionally used triton shells to make musical instruments for celebrations and ceremonies. As a result of overharvesting, tritons have become rare in many coral reefs.

Tritons eat another animal known as the crown-of-thorns starfish. These starfish eat coral polyps. Without living coral polyps to build the reef, all that eventually remains of a coral reef are the shells left by dead animals. In effect, a reef becomes a monument to what once lived there. In an effort to save coral reefs from the destruction caused by these starfish, several countries have laws that prohibit the collection of giant tritons. Sales of triton shell souvenirs are also discouraged.

In another type of relationship, an organism that has died still manages to provide a benefit to another organism. An example involves the giant triton, which is a snail that can grow as large as 20 inches (50 cm). Like all snails, the giant triton crawls along the seabed or coral rock with its muscular foot. Its soft body is protected by a beautiful shell. When a giant triton dies, its soft body slowly decays, leaving behind its hard shell. The shell, however, does not remain empty for long.

The shell is quickly claimed by a hermit crab. Unlike other crabs, a hermit crab cannot make a hard shell to protect its soft body. As a result, a hermit crab occupies the shell of a dead giant triton for protection.

Commensalism on a coral reef is usually not as obvious as a suckerfish getting a free ride on a manta ray or a hermit crab

A hermit crab uses a triton's shell for protection.

The sea sponge has been called a "living hotel" because several hundred tiny organisms may be living in it for protection.

occupying a giant triton's shell. Most of the relationships that are examples of commensalism involve small organisms that hide within larger organisms for protection. In fact, the larger organism may provide shelter for a number of smaller organisms. Sea sponges, for example, have many openings in which shrimp, worms, and other tiny organisms find protection.

Parasites

Some one-sided relationships found on a coral reef involve one organism benefiting at another organism's expense. This type of relationship is called **parasitism**. The organism that benefits is called the **parasite**. The other organism is known as the **host**. Most parasites are tiny organisms that live and feed on the body of their hosts. Fortunately, the reef has many cleaner shrimp that feed on the parasites, removing them before they have a chance to cause any serious damage to their hosts.

A sea cucumber releases a chemical that attracts a pearl fish. The pearl fish then enters the sea cucumber's body, where it feeds.

Some parasites, however, are not so tiny. The pearl fish is an example. This fish can grow to be as long as 25 inches (65 cm). Its body has either very small scales or none at all. This fish also lacks fins. As a result, its body is long, smooth, and slender. Pearl fish hunt for food during the night. Their days are spent living inside the body of another organism known as a sea cucumber. There, the pearl fish feeds on the sea cucumber. Such parasites as the pearl fish rarely kill their hosts. If they did, the parasites would no longer have a host to keep them alive.

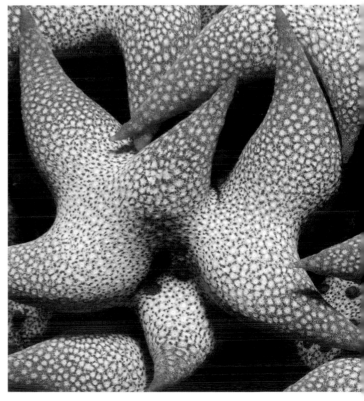

Algae found on reefs can grow to be 18 inches (45 cm) in length and resemble lettuce leaves.

Chapter Three

Feeding Relationships

All organisms need energy to survive. Energy is needed for movement, growth, repair, and reproduction. In addition, organisms need energy to carry out the basic tasks they must perform daily, such as digestion, circulation, and the elimination of wastes. The primary source of all this energy is the sun. Certain organisms on Earth are able to trap energy from the sun to use in photosynthesis. These organisms are known as **producers**. A

producer is an organism that uses energy from an outside source, such as the sun, to make food.

Some of the major producers found on a coral reef are among its smallest inhabitants. These include the tiny green algae that live inside polyps and giant clams. Green algae also form the slime that covers the coral rock left by dead polyps. These algae are believed to be responsible for making half the food produced on a coral reef. Not all green algae, however, are so small. Some grow quite large. These include green algae known as sea lettuce.

In addition to green algae, producers on a coral reef also include red algae and brown algae. Brown algae can grow to be as long as 325 feet (100 m). These long brown algae are known as kelp, which grow in bunches, or beds. Kelp beds provide shelter for many reef organisms. Seaweeds are also another type of algae that grow in coral reefs.

Another producer found on a coral reef is sea grass. Unlike algae, sea grasses are plants because they have roots, stems, and true leaves. Most sea grasses are found on the sandy bottoms of lagoons, while others grow on the coral rock left by dead polyps. Like kelp, sea grasses grow in beds in which many reef organisms find shelter. Some of these organisms, especially fish and turtles, depend on the sea grasses as their main source of food.

Food Additive

Red algae are the source of a food additive found in ice cream, canned foods, and bakery products.

Consumers

Producers use the food they make to get the energy they need to survive. Fortunately, producers make more food than they use. Much of what they do not use is eaten by **consumers**. A consumer is an organism that gets the energy it needs to survive by eating another organism.

Surgeonfish are among the most colorful consumers found on a coral reef. Their beautiful colors are reflected in their names, such as the yellowtail surgeonfish, the powderblue surgeonfish, and the lavender tang. Surgeonfish get their name from the extremely sharp spines located on each side of their tails. The spines are as sharp as a surgeon's scalpel. Surgeonfish use these sharp spines to chase other fish away from their food supply.

Surgeonfish have recently become a popular addition to saltwater aquariums because of their brilliant colors.

Their appearance has given sea urchins the title "pincushions of the sea."

Algae spread very quickly and can eventually cover a reef. If they do, the tiny coral polyps are smothered and slowly die, leaving nothing but coral rock. With their sharp, tiny teeth, surgeonfish scrape the algae from the coral and eat it. As a result, surgeonfish not only get the energy they need, they also keep a coral reef alive and healthy.

Fish are not the only reef organisms that eat producers. The sea urchin is another major consumer that depends on producers to get the energy it needs to live. Sea urchins have rounded bodies, often with spines sticking out.

Like surgeonfish, sea urchins play an important role in controlling the spread of algae. Sea urchins eat the tiny algae that grow on coral as well as the larger algae that grow as kelp and seaweed. In 1983, a disease killed 95 percent of the black, long-spined sea urchins living in the Florida and Caribbean reefs. Without these sea urchins, the algae spread unchecked. Large areas of the reefs slowly died as the polyps were smothered. Fortunately, these sea urchins are beginning to reappear in the Caribbean reefs.

Food Chains

Producers, such as algae and sea grasses, get energy from the food they make. Consumers, such as surgeonfish and sea urchins, get energy by eating the producers. Together, these organisms make up the first two links of a **food chain**. A food chain is a single pathway through which energy is passed from one organism to the next. Producers are always the first link in a food chain. Organisms that eat producers are known as **primary consumers**, which are the second link in a food chain.

Food chains usually include a third link known as a **secondary consumer**. A secondary consumer is an organism that eats a primary consumer. An example of a secondary consumer in a reef is the triggerfish.

The triggerfish has been known to attack divers that come too close to a nest of its eggs.

The dolphinfish is commonly called mahimahi. Despite its name, the dolphinfish is not related to the dolphin.

A Changing Role

Humans also eat triggerfish. When they do, they become the fourth link in the food chain.

Triggerfish eat sea urchins. Normally, the spines on a sea urchin's body protect it from being attacked or eaten. However, a triggerfish can shoot a powerful stream of water out its mouth to flip over a sea urchin and expose its soft underside. The triggerfish then uses its sharp teeth to feed on the sea urchin.

The triggerfish gets its name from the two spines located on top of its body. These spines can be locked together. When they are, the spines look like the trigger of a gun. By locking the two spines together, a triggerfish can wedge itself into a small opening on a reef. There, the triggerfish is protected from larger fish, such as a dolphinfish, that are trying to eat it.

If a dolphinfish succeeds in capturing and eating a triggerfish, it makes a fourth link in the food chain. In turn, the dolphinfish might be caught and serve as a meal for a human. A human would then make the fifth and final link in the food chain: algae–sea urchin–triggerfish–dolphinfish–human.

34

Food Webs

Feeding relationships are often complicated and cannot be described in terms of a food chain. Rather, a **food web** is used to show how energy is transferred between organisms as a result of their feeding relationships. A food web is a collection of food chains that are linked to one another.

Food webs can be very complex because they involve many different organisms. Even a simple food web may contain a wide variety of organisms. For example, the food web on the next page shows how eleven different organisms make up one simple food web on a coral reef. Notice places where the arrows cross one another. These show how some of the food chains are linked together to form a food web.

The **plankton** shown in this food web are small plants and animals that drift in the waters of a coral reef. Plant plankton are producers. All the other organisms in this food web are consumers, including the animal plankton. The arrows in a food web show how energy flows. For example, an arrow shows that animal plankton eat plant plankton. In turn, animal plankton are eaten by fan worms, blue damselfish, coral polyps, and sponges. Sponges are eaten by both sea slugs and angelfish. Angelfish are eaten by sharks, which also eat blue damselfish.

A food web can be used to predict what might happen if just one organism were removed from the reef for some reason. For example, if a disease were to kill most of the angelfish, then

Coral Reef Food Web

Spotted puffer fish

Whitetipped reef shark

Queen angelfish

Blue devil damsel

Masked butterfly fish

Sea slug

Split crown fan worm

Coral polyps

Tube sponge

Zooplankton

Plant plankton

the sharks would have to feed on more blue damselfish and butterfly fish. Their numbers would decrease. However, fewer angelfish would mean that the sea slugs would have more sponges to feed on. Therefore, the number of sea slugs would increase. More sea slugs would mean fewer coral polyps.

Although a food web describes feeding relationships, it does not show how much energy is actually transferred between organisms. As a rule, only about 10 percent of an organism's energy is transferred when one organism eats another. For example, an angelfish may get only 10 percent of the energy that is present in a sponge it eats. For this reason, there are rarely more than four links in any one food chain that is in a food web. There is just not enough energy to support more levels.

In addition to being protected by its hard body, this boxfish also secretes a powerful poison to ward off attackers.

Chapter Four

Survival Tactics

With so many organisms living on a coral reef, survival can be a challenge. Organisms not only have to compete for food, but they must also have some way of protecting themselves from being attacked and eaten. **Predators**, or organisms that feed on other organisms, are found everywhere on a reef.

Reef organisms use various tactics to avoid being eaten by predators. Many predators remain hidden during the day, venturing out only at night in search of

prey, or animals that serve as food. Even then, they must take care not to be eaten themselves.

Instead of hiding, some reef organisms make a display of themselves as a survival tactic. The cuttlefish is an example. When threatened, a cuttlefish will rapidly change its body colors, which flash in a striped pattern. A cuttlefish will also display its sharp beak to ward off a predator. If all this fails, it will release a cloud of ink to cover its retreat.

Many reef organisms have hardened exteriors, such as shells, that discourage predators. These include crabs, clams, mussels, oysters, turtles, lobsters, and fish whose bodies are covered with bony plates rather than scales.

Reef organisms with hardened exteriors often secrete poisons to ward off predators. An example is the fire coral. This organism is protected by a hard, sharp shell. Because fire coral has a fanlike structure and yellow, green, and brown colors, divers often mistake it for seaweed. Divers soon learn the difference when they brush against it. A fire coral has tentacles

The bumps that cover its body help make the cuttlefish look unappealing to predators.

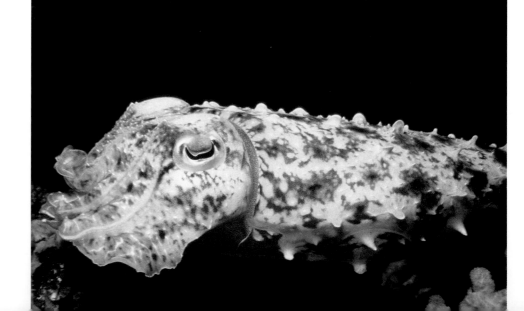

Although they resemble coral polyps, fire coral are more closely related to jellyfish.

that secrete a powerful poison. A diver can develop a burning sensation and stinging pain within five minutes of scraping against a fire coral.

Camouflage and Mimicry

Many reef organisms depend on their coloration to help them blend in with their surroundings. This camouflage protects them from predators. One of the most dangerous reef organisms is also one of the best at camouflaging itself. This is the stonefish, which has a body that is covered with bumps. Algae that grow on its body provide the camouflage. Buried in the seafloor, a stonefish can remain motionless and hidden for days. It blends in so well with the seafloor that a person wading through the reef may accidentally step on it. If that happens, the victim may suffer serious injury and possibly even die from the poison contained in the stonefish's fins.

Another survival tactic that reef organisms use is **mimicry**. Mimicry is the resemblance of one organism to another. This

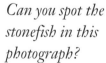
Can you spot the stonefish in this photograph?

The mimic octopus was discovered in 1998 by two underwater photographers in a coral reef near Indonesia.

resemblance may be in appearance, behavior, or both. One of the best examples of mimicry on a coral reef is displayed by the mimic octopus. This octopus changes its body shape, color, and the position of its tentacles so that it looks like an entirely different animal.

The mimic octopus can imitate or mimic a flounder, a sea snake, a jellyfish, a giant crab, a starfish, and several other reef animals. Some of these imitations make sense. For example, when the mimic octopus imitates a sea snake, which is very poisonous, other reef organisms will not try to eat it. However, no one is quite sure why the octopus bothers to mimic a flounder, which is harmless and serves as food for many other reef organisms.

Seeking Protection

Some reef organisms cannot protect themselves with hardened exteriors, poisons, bright colors, camouflage, or mimicry. In some cases, these organisms survive by gaining the protection of another organism. An example commonly found on a coral reef is shown by the behavior of the anemonefish. This fish get its name because it survives with the help of another organism known as a sea anemone. Related to the coral polyp, the sea anemone has a soft body with tentacles that surround its mouth.

The bright colors and swimming motions of anemonefish quickly attract the attention of other organisms that are searching for food. As a result, anemonefish make easy targets whenever they venture into open water. However, anemonefish rarely venture into open water. They spend almost all their time nestled among the tentacles of sea anemones. Anemonefish are not affected by the poisonous tentacles that sea anemones use to capture food. While anemonefish get protection, sea anemones benefit by having the colorful fish lure other organisms into their tentacles.

Many reef fish survive by seeking protection in numbers. These fish rarely travel alone, especially in daylight.

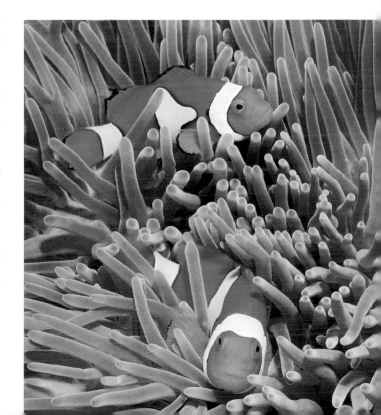

The relationship between an anemonefish and a sea anemone is a clear example of mutualism.

By traveling in a school, these catfish can deliver a powerful blow to any potential predator with their poisonous spines.

Changing Names

A school of fish was originally called a shoal of fish. A shoal is a shallow spot of water where fish gather. The word *shoal* was later changed to *school*.

Instead, they move about in a large group called a school that may consist of hundreds or even thousands of individuals of their own kind. The fish in a school stay together to seek protection, feed, move about, reproduce, and rest.

One of the largest schools seen in a coral reef consists of bluestriped snappers. These fish seek protection from larger fish by swimming together in a tight formation that moves as a unit. The school appears to be one giant fish whose size wards off any potential attacker. If they are attacked, the fish quickly disperse in all directions. The predator may be momentarily confused, allowing the snappers to escape and regroup.

Another fish that seeks protection in a school is the striped eel catfish. This is the only catfish living in coral reefs that can cause a painful sting with the sharp spines on its fins. A school of these catfish moves forward like a steamroller. Those in front swim downward and toward the rear of the school. Those just behind take their place and then do the same. In this way, the catfish in the school take turns searching the seafloor for small crabs and other food.

Multiple Defenses

Most reef organisms depend on one tactic to survive. However, there are some reef organisms, such as the commensal shrimp, that use multiple tactics. This shrimp's survival tactics include having a hardened exterior, a body that can change color to match its surroundings, and sharp pincers. In addition, the commensal shrimp is usually found seeking protection among the spines of a sea urchin. As its name implies, the commensal shrimp benefits from this relationship, while the sea urchin is not affected in any way.

The relationship between this shrimp and sea urchin is an example of commensalism.

The porcupine fish's teeth are sharp enough to break open the shells of clams, crabs, and other reef organisms.

One of the more interesting reef organisms with multiple survival tactics is the porcupine fish. As its name suggests, this fish's body is covered with scales that can stick out like the spines on a porcupine. The fish takes in air or water to inflate its body so that its spines stick out. A porcupine fish can grow to be as long as 18 inches (45 cm), and can double its size when inflated. This can scare off a predator and make it too big for

another organism to swallow it. Even if a predator is willing to take the chance, the porcupine fish can protect itself with its sharp teeth and the poison stored in its skin.

This starfish usually feeds on polyps twice a day for several hours each time.

Chapter Five

A Fragile Structure

Despite being the largest and most impressive structures made by living things, coral reefs are fragile. A reef will grow only in specific conditions that are met in shallow tropical seas. If the water conditions change even slightly, a reef might not be able to grow and may even start to die.

From time to time, water conditions in reef areas change. These changes may be the result of natural causes. For example, such storms as hurricanes and

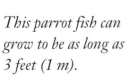

Tiny Eaters

When it is six months old, a crown-of-thorns starfish is less than 0.5 inch (1 cm) in size, but it is already feasting on polyps.

typhoons can stir up huge waves that break apart a coral reef. Heavy rains from the storms can dilute the water so that not enough calcium carbonate remains for polyps to build a reef. In addition, changes in water currents can smother a reef with mud. Without sunlight, the reef will slowly die because its algae can no longer carry out photosynthesis.

Predators

Natural predators can also destroy a reef. Two such predators are the crown-of-thorns starfish and the parrot fish. The crown-of-thorns starfish can grow to be as long as 12 inches (30 cm) across and have as many as twenty arms that are covered with poisonous spines. As it spreads its arms across a section of coral, the starfish pushes its stomach out through its mouth. It then secretes digestive fluids that turn polyps into a "soup" the starfish sucks into its stomach. In one year, a single starfish can destroy a reef area up to 180 times its own size. Because these starfish reproduce in such large numbers, they can quickly populate and then destroy a reef.

This parrot fish can grow to be as long as 3 feet (1 m).

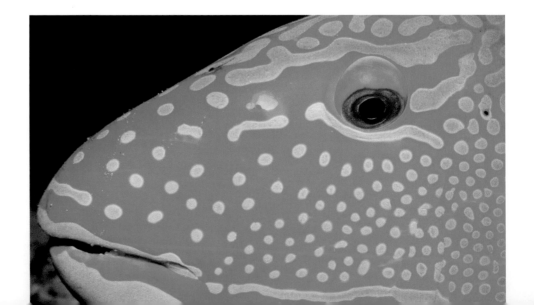

Parrot fish get their name from their teeth, which are fused into a single beaklike structure. As primary consumers, parrot fish use this structure to scrape and eat the algae that grows on coral. While feeding on the algae, parrot fish often take bites out of the coral. They grind up the coral, consuming the algae living inside the polyps. When they are finished feeding, parrot fish excrete a sandy substance that once was living coral. A single parrot fish can grind up enough coral in a year to produce one ton of sand.

Human Impact

Humans have also been responsible for the destruction of coral reefs. Scientists have gathered evidence that indicates that reefs found in ninety-three countries have been damaged by human activities. Scientists also estimate that humans have destroyed more than 35 million acres (14 million hectares) of reefs over the past few decades. At this rate, nearly 70 percent of the world's reefs will be destroyed within our lifetimes.

One cause of this destruction is pollution. In some cases, humans have polluted the waters directly by dumping sewage near coral reefs. Oil spills and the discharge of chemicals have also polluted the waters. Reefs in the Middle East have been especially affected by oil spills.

Human activities have also led indirectly to the pollution of reef areas. As more and more tourists visit the reefs, the construction of resorts, restaurants, shopping areas, and marinas has steadily progressed. This construction causes soil to erode.

Garbage
Reef animals have been seen seeking protection in empty cans, old teapots, and even refrigerators that humans have tossed into the water.

Mangroves are tropical trees and bushes that are believed to have once stretched along almost 70 percent of the shorelines near coral reefs.

The soil eventually finds its way into reef waters, making the water cloudy and smothering the coral polyps. Mangrove forests located along the shore normally filter the soil out of runoff before it reaches the reef waters. However, these forests are being cut down to provide tourists with sandy beaches that overlook the reefs.

Reefs near urban areas have been affected mainly by chemical pollution. Chemicals in fertilizers and insecticides applied to crops and flowers on land eventually wind up in reef waters. Some of these chemicals are used for food by the algae that live on a reef. With so much food available, these algae quickly reproduce. Consumers that eat the algae cannot keep up with their rapid growth. As a result, the algae smother and slowly destroy the reef.

No More Fish

On some reefs, there are few fish to be seen. Once again, humans have been partly responsible. In some cases, over fishing has simply wiped out the fish populations. To meet a growing demand for food, some fishers have resorted to using methods for catching as many fish as possible in a short time. This includes the use of trap nets. These nets catch not only fish but also other reef organisms, such as sharks, dolphins, manta rays, and turtles. Instead of being released back into the waters, these animals are often discarded and eventually die. Even if they are released, these animals may have been injured and can no longer survive on their own.

Another method is called fish bombing. Some fishers, especially in Southeast Asia, detonate such explosives as dynamite and homemade bombs to kill large numbers of fish. Obviously, these explosions destroy the reefs as well. Still another method used to catch fish involves poisons, such as cyanide.

Widespread Bleaching

In 1998, coral reefs around the world experienced the most extensive and severe bleaching in history. Coral bleaching was reported in sixty countries.

Cyanide Fishing

At one time, cyanide fishing was used to capture tropical fish for aquarium shops. However, the demand for live fish in restaurants has led to the increased use of cyanide fishing in many reef areas. Divers spray the poison at a fish, which is temporarily stunned but not killed. Although the poison is not concentrated enough to kill the fish, it is powerful enough to kill coral polyps and other tiny reef organisms living nearby. Each year, about 175 tons of cyanide are sprayed on the reefs in the Philippines.

Other Causes

Humans have destroyed reefs in still other ways. They have removed coral from reefs for both decorative and construction purposes. Even dead coral makes an attractive item to display. Coral rock can be turned into lime, a material that is used in construction.

Visitors to reef areas often do not take the time or care to prevent damage. Boaters drop anchors directly onto coral reefs, waders walk on reefs, and swimmers break off pieces of live coral as souvenirs.

The final blow humans may deliver to coral reefs is **global warming**. Global warming is caused by gases, such as carbon dioxide, that are released through the burning of fuels. These gases collect in the atmosphere above Earth. These gases trap sunlight, causing the Earth's temperature to increase. Coral reefs are extremely sensitive to temperature changes. An average increase in water temperature of just 1° Fahrenheit over the course of two to three days can kill the algae that live inside polyps. The death of the colorful algae leaves only the colorless polyps. In turn, they too will die, leaving only white, lifeless coral rock.

Aware of how both nature and humans have caused severe reef destruction, international organizations and national governments have devoted resources to stopping the damage before it is too late. Hopefully, their efforts will save the most impressive structures ever made by living things.

Limestone, which is the same substance as is found in coral rock, was used to build the Empire State Building in New York City.

52

Glossary

algae—plantlike organisms that grow in both freshwater and salt water, including coral reefs

atoll—island made of reefs that surround a body of water

barrier reef—reef that is found far from shore

biodiversity—variety of life that is found in a particular area

commensalism—relationship between two organisms in which one benefits and the other is not affected in any way

consumer—organism that gets the energy it needs to survive by eating another organism

coral reef—ridge of rocky material just beneath the surface of a tropical sea that has been made by living things

food chain—single pathway through which energy is passed from one organism to the next

food web—collection of food chains that are linked to one another

fringing reef—reef that is fairly narrow and develops near the shore

global warming—gradual warming of Earth, including its waters

habitat—place where an organism lives

host—organism that serves to benefit another organism

mimicry—resemblance of one organism to another in either appearance or behavior

mutualism—relationship between two organisms in which both benefit

organism—living thing

parasite—organism that benefits at the expense of another organism

parasitism—relationship between two organisms in which one benefits at the expense of the other

photosynthesis—process used by algae and plants to make foods

plankton—small plants and animals that drift in the water

polyp—tiny, soft-bodied living thing that is primarily responsible for building a coral reef

predator—organism that feeds on another animal

prey—organism that serves as a food source for another organism

primary consumer—organism that eats producers

producer—organism that uses energy from an outside source, such as the sun, to make food

secondary consumer—organism that eats primary consumers

sessile—staying in one place

To Find
Out More

Books

Albet, Toni. *The Incredible Coral Reef*. Trickle Creek Books, 2001.

Ferrari, Andrea and Antonella Ferrari. *Reef Life*. Firefly Books, 2002.

Galko, Francine. *Coral Reef Animals*. Heinemann Library, 2002.

Ganeri, Anita. *Coral Reefs*. Peter Bedrick Books, 2001.

Green, Jen. *A Coral Reef*. Crabtree Publishing, 2002.

Tackett, Denise Nielsen and Larry Tackett. *Reef Life*. Microcosm Limited, 2002.

Organizations and Online Sites

J.L. Scott Marine Education Center & Aquarium
115 Beach Boulevard
Biloxi, MS 39530
http://www.aquarium.usm.edu/coralreef/
This site contains a wealth of information, all available in Portable Document Format (PDF). The information is organized into the following sections: Introduction, What Are Corals?, How Do Corals Reproduce and Grow?, Where Are Coral Reefs Found?, Life on a Coral Reef, and Conservation of Coral Reefs. You can also click on Resources and References.

Reef Education Network
http://www.reef.edu.au/
You can create your own notebook as you explore this site, which contains a Who's Who that includes information and photographs about reef organisms. Click on whatever you want to add to your notebook, which is saved and available whenever you return to this site.

Reef Relief
http://www.reefrelief.org/kids/
Learn what you can do to help protect coral reefs.

Coral Reef Links
http://www.response.restoration.noaa.gov/oilaids/coral/links.html
Scroll down to "Sites for Kids" and find "25 Things You Can Do To Save Coral Reefs."

The Coral Kingdom
http://www.photolib.noaa.gov/reef/index.html
This site contains a large collection of photos of coral reef organisms from around the world. Animals are grouped according to vertebrates, or those with backbones, and invertebrates, or those without backbones.

National Wildlife Federation
http://www.nwf.org/productions/coralreef/
You can learn more about threats to reefs and what is being done to protect them from further damage. You can also watch a trailer for a 42-minute film that is called Coral Reef Adventure, which takes viewers to coral reefs in the South Pacific.

American Museum of Natural History
http://www.amnh.org/nationalcenter/kids/kids_bio/articles.html
Learn why coral reefs are called the rain forests of the sea. A link takes you to the website of the Planetary Coral Reef Foundation.

A Note on Sources

This book proved to be one of the more challenging ones I have written because of the wealth of information available on coral reefs. With such rich biodiversity, coral reefs provide so much to write about that it is difficult to know where to begin and what to cover. Before I even began to write, I had to decide how to organize the material so the reader would find a theme for each chapter.

Once I chose a theme for each chapter, I searched for interesting organisms that I could use as illustrative examples. Two books proved particularly valuable. Both are titled *Reef Life*. One was written by Andrea and Antonella Ferrari. This book has hundreds of colorful photographs of reef organisms and a brief description of each one. The other book, written by Denise and Larry Tackett, was most helpful in that it, too, deals with scientific concepts that are strikingly illustrated on a reef.

These two books had more than enough examples to use for each chapter. My next step was to search the Internet for more detailed information about each organism I selected. As is often the case, the number of "hits" could be overwhelming. Therefore, I conducted my search by using the scientific names of the organisms, which are conveniently provided in the book written by the Ferraris.

One source I wish I had as I was writing this book was first-hand experience. Hopefully, I'll get that chance someday.

—*Salvatore Tocci*

Index

Numbers in *italics* indicate illustrations.

About the Author

Salvatore Tocci taught high school and college science for almost thirty years. He has a bachelor's degree from Cornell University and a Master of Philosophy degree from The City University of New York.

He has written books that deal with a range of science topics, from biographies about famous scientists to a high school chemistry textbook. He has also traveled throughout the United States to present workshops at national science conventions to show teachers how to emphasize the applications of scientific knowledge to students in their everyday lives.

Tocci lives in East Hampton, New York, with his wife Patti. Both retired from teaching, they spend their leisure time sailing and traveling. One trip they plan to take in the near future is to the Great Barrier Reef.